I, BIRD

Róisín Ní Neachtain is a writer and artist living in Kildare. She was awarded the Dennis O'Driscoll Literary Bursary Award for Established Writers in 2025, second place at the Red Line and third place at the Maria Edgeworth Competition. Her work has also been shortlisted with Write by the Sea, The Aryamati Poetry Prize for chapbooks and the Fish Publishing Poetry Competition. She has been mentored by Enda Wyley and, in her painting practice, by Brian Maguire.

ISBN: 978-1-917617-48-2

Cover designed by Aaron Kent

Edited and Typeset by Aaron Kent

Broken Sleep Books Ltd
PO BOX 102
Llandysul
SA44 9BG

I, bird is an extraordinary collection of poems that explores the interior landscapes of the mind, the thresholds that confine us, and the imaginative spaces that shift and shape perspectives in ways that allow us to notice 'the glow of lights from small places.' Language is made strange in *I, bird* – Ní Neachtain never goes the expectant route, enticing the reader instead to stay alert, to stay awake to its possibilities, its twist and turns, where one word is 'the colour of desire' and another 'the shimmer-green of long grasses.' These remarkable poems speak of grief, myth, the body, and of 'tarnished metaphor', and Ní Neachtain is brilliantly attuned to pattern, weaving these themes throughout the collection to give the book a sense of enthralling cohesion that will make you want to read it all at once before returning to the beginning, to start again.

— Leeanne Quinn

In this intimate, philosophical collection, Róisín Ní Neachtain confronts the horror of having a mind and a body, interrogating what to do with each in a world of cruel and unjust inequalities. Can a mind transcend the limitations socially imposed upon a body? Can language? What can a person do when cleanliness belies harm? For all her questioning, Ní Neachtain also offers us answers. 'You look around the room again and decide that you can make it dirty too.' *I, bird* is probing, existential, and visceral.

— Gustav Parker Hibbett

These are extraordinary poems by a necessary new voice: simultaneously surreal, poised, playful, harrowing. At once walled in and pushing against their structures, these poems erode and are re-sculpted through this impressive collection, taking flight as they find new forms. Quite simply, 'Listen to these fragments.'

— Francesca Bratton

Amidst the climate disaster, in *I, bird* Róisín dares us to find solace in roots, trees, and birds, to find communion in and with wilderness, pouring 'the water of vowels' into our mouths, fulfilling her poetic interest in 'what has been carved out'. *I, bird* embodies and defies nature: Róisín's poems are precise like a score with surrendering moments of delight and revelation. *I, bird* is a performance and an invitation to look beyond the human because 'there is life outside'.

— Rafael Mendes

Like a contemporary, clear-eyed, Irish Baudelaire, Róisín Ní Neachtain's *I, bird* wages a war on wholeness. The prose poems and wounded lyrics of this collection '[spit] venom', uncovering for us the abject in the lush. With a lyricism that is cool, caustic, and elliptical – 'the grief of a sea noise' – Ní Neachtain's poetry wrenches human dignity from a barbarous world.
— Clíodhna Bhreatnach

The poems move from the interior to the outside world, deftly and with precision. From 'The floor feels soft. The floor is not comforting' to 'Out of her mouth flew a small bird'. These are tender, lyrical poems. Ní Neachtain has a unique way of seeing the world – a mesmerising way of showing it to us. A gifted and welcome voice.
— Martina Dalton

Róisín Ní Neachtain's practice as a visual artist infuses her poetry with colour, light, and synaesthetic imagery. In a combination of prose and free-form poems, *I, bird* destabilises reality, conjuring aspects of David Lynch and Marina Abramović. This is a collection for our times – 'genocide is being perpetrated in a foreign land ... Now is the time for the 'Screaming Tree' ('The White Room').
— Amanda Bell

CONTENTS

THE WHITE ROOM *MEDUSA*   11

EURYDICE SURVIVES ORPHEUS   30

GRIEF   31

THE SUN WOULD BE GOLD AGAIN   33

I SEE YOU KNEW MY SMALL BETRAYAL   35

BLUE TREE   36

SAY A THING   37

I, BIRD   39

NIOBE GRIEVES HER CHILDREN   40

AS LIGHT SPEAKS SOUNDLESS   48

FOR THE WOMEN WHO COULD NOT INVOKE RIVER GODS
TO BECOME LAUREL TREES...   62

ACKNOWLEDGEMENTS   67

This book is dedicated to University College Dublin,
a place of dreams and futures which saved me three times.

I, bird

Róisín Ní Neachtain

Broken Sleep Books

THE WHITE ROOM *MEDUSA*

This is a square, empty room in which there is one window. You can't see a door and you have no idea how you got in. The window is too small to have entered through. You are not in your usual clothes but it's not in a straitjacket either. You find no relief in this. You are frozen against the floor. The floor is strangely soft but provides you with no comfort. This is a clinical space and not the type of hospital you have been forced to stay in. For a moment you think it is no different to White Cube. This isn't a hospital. This is not an experiment. You are part of an exhibition. You are the exhibition. All eyes are on you and you must perform.

It would be something not to perform. It would be something to lie here perfectly still and immobile, both in body and mind. You would not think about solitary confinement. You would not recite poetry in your head. You would not try to count time. You would not try to stay sane. How different would it be from outside of these walls really?

Don't think about what you might have done to end up here. Focus on that window and its perfect, crisp shape. There is life outside. There are laws of nature. The weakest gets killed off, devoured. What is left of its flesh is left to rot. There are anemones, daisies and roses. Think of all those lush blooms which are productive, even in their decay. In their decay, they are fed from. They nourish the earth. The worms feed off them. Seeds take hold. Seeds take root.

This is what you must think about now. Roots. There is a tree outside that window. Perhaps an oak tree like the one from your childhood garden. Perhaps there is a swing attached to a strong branch. Perhaps children play on it and are safe.

What is around that oak tree on which there are no leaves? There is ivy that winds around its large trunk. More life. For a moment, you consider the symbiosis of the life outside that window. That one tree has its insects, its nests, its birds. It has its own light, its own shadows. It has its own music. Now you wonder how you can really know what a moment is since there is no sense at all of the passage of time.

Is there anything else outside, beyond that tree? Who is there?

Let me tell you a story about that place. There are no children there. It is merely the oak tree where lovers meet to quarrel. Women go there to scream too. This is the Screaming Tree. A woman might be raped, climb to that tree and scream and the tree might take it all in. Calm as anything, all laid back. The bark will remain stoic. And don't forget that there are no leaves to tremble. The earth will not shake.

Don't be shocked now. We all need a place outside to scream. You couldn't possibly expect women to scream inside. In the kitchen. In the bedroom. In the bed she shares with the man who provides for her. By the crib of their babies.

There is a genocide being perpetrated in a foreign land. You have seen the bloody bodies of children being carried through streets. You have seen a man carry the body parts of his infant child in a bag and lay them out on the earth of his stolen land. You can't look anymore. You can't read the details. You can't sit here and cry all day. Crying your useless, fucking tears that mean nothing to these people. Now is the time for the Screaming Tree.

Jane and Jack go the Screaming Tree to quarrel too. They don't fight at home. Jack is a lawyer and Jane is an interior decorator and it really doesn't do to fight at home. After all, somebody might hear them. People might *talk*. At the Screaming Tree, Jack can be a dickhead and a woman can be foul-mouthed. Jack might even like her being a bitch in the wrong sort of ways. At home, it might be uncomfortable. It might make him squirm. But not at the Screaming Tree where it could even be a turn-on. He might get to slap her a bit and she might scream a bit louder then.

I wouldn't think too much about that place if I were you but *for a moment* it was *nice* to think that it might be a different sort of place to this white room.

What are the smells here? What can you feel?

You are still on the floor. The floor feels soft. The soft floor is not comforting.

How heavy you feel. How heavy your limbs feel. This white room is a lie. White is a lie. White is not pure or soft or clean. White is not healing. White is open and not intimate. Scream it now. **THIS WHITE IS NOT IMMACULATE**. How stark and cruel it is in its clarity. Safe menace. A fucking hangover migraine.

Look outside that window again. What is there now?

There is no Screaming Tree now. There is no place for people to unleash their fury and sadness. There is only some pretty, chocolate box cover poster. Flat fields which are too beautiful and flowers of all the colours of the rainbow being too perfect. The sun shines bright but not in a way which makes anybody squint. There are barely enough clouds in that sky to break up the monotony of that pristine blue which fades on the horizon into a starry night where the moon radiates an unnatural iridescence and glowers into darkness to make you shudder a bit. The air there has no movement though. There is no breeze to tell you that you are still alive, no biting wind to gulp down or rain to make you run faster.

But, of course, this is only a poster. What you really want to know is what is behind it.

I can tell you now that it is a void. A black hole where people and their small emotions and tedious lives disappear. The black hole does not differentiate between the good and bad. It can't tell whether you're a good woman who worked hard and didn't deserve to be murdered in that back alley behind their office for a couple of dollars and their fake Louis Vuitton handbag or whether you were that CEO who fucked all his secretaries behind his pretty wife's back, laid off thousands of people and caused a dozen suicides. Black Hole doesn't care.

Don't forget where you are. Let us get back once again to this room. What are the noises here?

You consider saying something aloud to create a noise here. You make a small, tentative squeak because you wonder if you still have a voice. You make another sound. You sing *happy fucking birthday* and clap in the way that made your dog bark and snarl.

You have grey hair. As a woman with grey hair, you are now invisible. You are invisible in a square, empty room in which there is a crisp, perfect, clinical window. You have hazel eyes which are too wide for your face. You have small, thin lips which are too small for your face. You are not a natural beauty and because you are not a natural beauty, women tend to like you and men dismiss you. You neither have the humour or intelligence to make up for the lack of your physical charms. You are an ordinary woman. You are an ordinary woman whom people have never minded.

You decide now to sit up and pull your trousers up to stare at the stubble on your legs. You realise the only smell here is you. It's your piss. You are the unclean thing here. You have pissed yourself in your sleep from fear. This does not worry you. You accept it because you have often pissed yourself from fear.

You look around the room again and decide that you can make it dirty too. You can pick holes in those walls and pick out the filling and from that filling you can make objects.

.

EURYDICE SURVIVES ORPHEUS

GRIEF

When I was born, my godmother blessed me with her breath. This makes me think of the birth of Picasso – the uncle who exhaled cigar smoke on a newborn and forced his lungs to open. Though perhaps that story is a myth. I wonder why my godmother thought her "souffle" was a blessing.

Now her mind is fractured. She looks for words between seismic shifts and black holes.

even as I write this I tremble, my fingers thick-honeyed and humming against my pen. I count half-tones between each syllable. each fragment engaged and flexed, grasping wisps that flirt against flesh.

At night, we run through graves and leap wrong. I was never much for long-jumping. The mechanics never did quite work for me. For me. Me. Me. The anthem of a soliloquy.

We are loose-boned in this night.

We fly between constellations of others. Violent dusks.

Where there is nothing. Nothing above the sickness of a dying mind.

What could be more violent than a will fighting against a broken body and mind? Minds have broken long before lungs. Before tears bristled on mouths.

We are felt in stillness and in noise.

Break rock and bleed indigo silhouette.

THE SUN WOULD BE GOLD AGAIN

I see it is over us

and spread like an oppressive firmament

and some cool, sticky substance

across the way we were,

the want-to-talk,

the emergency of holding

each other up into the fight of flesh.

I see that absence of the personal way –

meaning that you are no longer calligraphy

of my low ideals or austere idylls.

Real as verbena, dropseed

and the misconduct of a dahlia,

curve-petalled away from touch,

you press a heavy weight into my chest

to make me learn different ways

of knowing home

and beat about the obvious word of confession –

pretend to believe in other sad things –

the coal-crying of the plundered earth

or the cracked bones of a dog flung from a car.

I see it impossibly –

you would not make it another year

and I would be vicious-tongued,

lash into the last of you,

beg you to let me slip over

and trespass your body

so I would not run

from the death-devourer of men

and the sun would be gold again

and shine

on your alive skin.

I SEE YOU KNEW MY SMALL BETRAYAL
after reading Henri Cole

There are cobalt beetles in the fertile soil and the darkness of a liqueur seeping into it which is the almost-belief in your love. I am elated, brighter than a sting and pink against the nocturnal dunes on this beach. *We are ruins. We are ruins. We are ruins.* You say this over and over against my half-shaven arm and I do not understand you in the right way. I do not feel your tears or ask you why you are heavy and hollow against me. You are revealed as you will be later, enamelled skin in a coffin with your dark hair brushed in a way you would have hated. I imagine this because I was not there and did not hold you and still think your death is a cruel deceit. I do not listen and do not see and do not see so I suck my stomach in and lie: *rest against me* – and vaguely feel the quiver of my blindness. I feel the cost of coldness now, how you knew my small betrayal but still smiled against my breast.

BLUE TREE

Why, they ask, do I order them about here, all high-handed? Look at this broken thing. It's less fragile now. Listen to these fragments. Take one up and make a cut with it across that blue field there. Don't dip it in the paints. Don't be tempted to lick them. Perhaps you could make a chain of these fragments, a mosaic necklace. Here is a tear now. You see! Look again! You did that when you cut that slate off on the horizon. Why is blue the colour of desire and such a soft thing? Why does he look at me like that? Green never does. Shimmer-green of long grasses. Cooling and shading against my legs in the end of the too-high summer. Always crying that lilac eye of the sky. Always too hurt to stay still in the perfect curve of that part of the distance. He's too smooth. Eroded and sculpted by all my little fantasies. All artists do this. Inflict that damage instead to the great red blister firing up above us. Blue is all longing and the lust of water. Blue not like that dangerous part of flames or those flecks of your eye you inherited from your father. Stir up that cobalt and indigo - how you love that indigo - and make of it a fine tree. See now, Blue Tree. Blue Tree on the orange sand of childhood. Blue Tree like all the trees we need to breathe. I might press my lips to your bark now and make a tender wound in my mouth from which I whisper only cornflower, azure, cyan, turquoise… Be Midnight Blue Tree for a moment now while I tell you all ultramarine is blinding bright to that invisible tongue which carries the imprint of the bark from Blue Tree on the Orange Sand of Childhood. Much too soon, he says, for a coarse splinter of wood to form an anchor for me in the dark form of the sky.

SAY A THING

You're sitting here in some unknown place by a wall and after a few cigarettes, you start wondering what is on the other side. Here, there is no place for beauty and no place to hide. And yet you will forever be woman and so you are also unseen, bleeding and wiping the tears of someone who is dying at the wrong time. On the other side, maybe there is somebody like you who can stop at a tree in the morning and say a thing which might be carved into it, which might be remembered. Something like how you loved the movement of a song hummed into the veins of your child and that might have made them live if they'd been born on that other side of the wall and that you don't watch lights which are too bright or stare at the nicotine-stained fingers which touch the folded skin of your stomach and bring you into their orbit. There are paler things than you which breathe into fresh graves and tend to tulip bulbs and dirt, pour the water of death into small talk and make you into a gilded cut rocked from the sky. Believe me when I say there is no separation or hunger between these roots, yours and mine. We will both unravel and be wrath. We will be sick bone fed to dogs and push the ugly changes of our bodies to a tarnished metaphor.

For class, I read Egg/Shell by Victoria Kennefick, Obit by Victoria Chang and Grief is the Thing with Feathers by Max Porter.

I have watched a documentary about Michael Longley and can't stop thinking about his collection of eggshells and how, at times, he takes the swan's eggshell out and just holds it with both hands.

I write. I, bird, write.

I, BIRD

Little things are growing broken from my lover's skull and sometime in December 2024, I wake up and realise that I am not in my body. My body is there below me but is not slumped unconscious or dead. It is living on and remembering how to be quiet. It is breathing and unaware of this complication. Of the detachment of a wild bird from its house. I, bird, do not caw in anxiety. I, crow, I, sparrow, I, eagle, I, vulture – cartwheel and leap out to peck at the flesh of tidy spaces and tidy people who are too well arranged. I am ready to have my own words and not be rejected by a form of parasite which sucks from the flesh of a heart but will not hold its secrets. Words which remind me in some new place of damp feathers and their punk-spiked scent. I can be bird that you actually like and anchor driftwood-confusion, ferry elegies and final noises. There is a sheen to the pitch-black horror of my plumage which refracts and is not terrible female. Female like mother which cuts the bloom from a stalk to make an ornamental nest and stop us going beyond. Claw your way to flight now, hope. Fan yourself out, corpse. Tell me that my sticky, wet eye is not ringing fury or the grief of a sea noise which harnesses defiance.

NIOBE GRIEVES HER CHILDREN

In January 2025, I wake up off the coast of Algeria. I have flown over deserts and taken shelter from sandstorms. I notice, at these times, the glow of lights from small places. Inside. I have stopped looking through windows. I have stopped looking for my body and no longer wonder about the length of my hair or whether I have more wrinkles around my eyes and whether that should be celebrated. I think of the poetry I wrote, in my human shape, about Clytemnestra. I made her hair long and tressed it to make a ladder for the devil. Agamemnon climbed up her hair and took their daughter's life to sail on for a man's war. Agamemnon could not survive this.

During my travels, I gather empty eggshells abandoned at the bottom of trees or at the edge of sea cliffs and bring them to a solitary place where few people venture. I name them as my children and count the tears they would have cried when asking me for food. I count time and calculate the journeys I would have to take to forage for them. This makes eating alone easier. Sometimes, as I eat, I imagine rationing the portions for them. One bite for me, one bite for you.

Vrooom, vrooom, vroom, here comes the plane. Ahhhhh, aahhh, yum. YUMMM. Isn't that so good?

Recently, an eagle of singular stupidity tried to mate with me and told me I did not have to collect empty eggshells. I could be real mother soon. He did not understand that I am only interested in what was once full. I want what has been carved out.

In April 2025, ghosts of birds are born from the empty shells and they come to me. They understand that I can give them new air. I breathe into their spaces. Here is *word, word, word. Take my language.* I hear them now with their beautiful, ghostly noises. They, endlessly, want more from me and I, exhausted, want to give it. Unlike birds of flesh, we fly straight away and look for a new home. I decide that I quite like the idea of the Amazon. I have spent enough time over arid lands and in the mountains of Asia. It is true that we do not have to worry about weather patterns or the change of seasons and this makes life easier. Because we are not seen by other animals, we are safer. I do not have to weep. I do not have to chase predators.

Little things are flourishing from my lover's skull and I will come to collect them soon.

On our way to Peru, we see a line of graves with small, wooden crosses and I decide to bury some seeds there. Trees will grow from them and I will visit these in a few years, make new nests. New spaces for the undead, a place of harmonies and collisions.

I realise that one of my ghost-birds is a phoenix. There is no other explanation. Every fortnight, I see her in flames and, soon after, she is reborn. She will always need me more. The other birds are growing steadily and look for the water of vowels and the fleshy consonants that I can give them. *One more word. One more letter. One more story of a boy flying around on a magic carpet and rubbing lamps to makes some wishes come true. Are the wishes worthy? Is the boy? Find out tomorrow and tomorrow and tomorrow, my little ghost-bird loves. I do not want you to know the fate of wishes yet.*

Sometime in Autumn of 2026, my ghost-birds fly off, each with a letter of their own, each with an idea to form their own nests from, leaving trails of bleeding ink and discarding feathers and parts of hearts. Phoenix-bird is still here. Still bursting into flames and being reformed into a bald, scrawny, gossamer chick. Endless newborn. No sooner does one feather appear but it is gone. She is immediate and urgent. In the other place, she would be the raw pink and red of a fresh hatch with shrivelled skin and black, bulging, embryonic eyes, not ready to see the world. Here, she is translucent and is doomed to be that ugly half-there and eternally new and in death.

I do not reveal the names of my birds to you.

I only whisper them into the eggshells that they left behind.

AS LIGHT SPEAKS SOUNDLESS
after Iphigenia's sacrifice, from her mother's perspective

As light speaks soundless

I can still see you

it is no longer your name

                                          that grows eyes

green-mirrored

 stone clean burdened

                              and tells me where to make

                    water

home

too night to a thousand open suns

                                   with all my words driven into
veins

look on my lips more than a grave's
blue grace

a child once made a shape
in the sands outside my house

see sea-stars

you're no more than a wound of years

where

love grew blindness

each memory is

below

I fall

and aching hour I left lung
to be stacked into a fire's fissure

count count count count cunt

your mouth was shut when you drank wrote inhaled lied wrote

sang

my years and refuge

was a book

was a passing

was a line   alone   a

man

                                                                who

knew what language was where my hands would play into a dance
play into an earth call my doors to empty to name to windows to
letters

younger

than the vanity of my hair

tressed to make a ladder

for the devil

in breath-vacuums I found

a single vowel spat venom

in my breast I sheltered a sound

quiet for the strange bare glare of your gait

before a drunk man

was heavy was never grief was never man was never red

how did I speak before a winter emerged on my tongue?

now it is shy

echo

who who

ego

at my face

and between my teeth

and between grey holds and a hanged flower where a bird would
nest

and

I hear you ask —

did the bird have the violence of colours?

sometimes and the suns were jealous and the oceans were jealous
and if the mountains were jealous

they would call a claw to clip

its feathers and drown them in a ploughed

droughted

riverbed

taste its flutter its later truth

and the same nothing which is time which is treeless beauty

the crooked timber which is guest of a mud recess

the same feathers which were pink and orange and yellow and purple and all the colours of a refracted prism where light reveals its skin and pushes its blood to cloth and pushes its silvered shadows to chasm *and did the bird die by the violence of colours?*

                                        the bird
died

death

and sang no more

a child

once made a shape in the snow

outside

my house

is

                                    a
                            winged crimson
                                      sight

it sees

like God

In a dream, I stop to see a woman being caught in a violent wind. Around her everything was still and yet this woman was being swept and tossed around by the force of a hurricane. She was screaming and, as she howled, her hair lifted in the wind and flew into her mouth to suffocate her.

O mercy! O mercy! I thought she said as she begged me to reach towards her and with both hands grab the rope that her hair had become and tug it out of her.

Where were the people around me? Could they not see that the wind was trying to murder this woman? And what if I didn't pull the rope from her? What if I climbed down inside her? And in her bowels found another life?

O mercy and mercy, I will take your hair from your body and let you live said some other voice that didn't quite belong to me. So I pulled and pulled and pulled her ruby tresses glistening from the insides of her and the wind howled at me in anger.

When all the hair had been removed, she stayed immobile, her mouth agape. Her eyes had frozen over in horror. Her hands were clenched.

I thought that prayers from darkness would be less humiliated than a daylight anger.

No sound now came from her.

The wind is a murderer.

When dawn struck at that moment, her tongue moved forward. Out of her mouth flew a small bird of such powerful blues and greens that I screamed and shook. Language, music and numbers. Yes, I had seen colour in all of these but never in an animal.

The bird flew by me and straight up into the sky, it seemed to weep its song for the whole of the Earth.

I turned briefly to see the woman's body shatter into crimson dust.

FOR THE WOMEN WHO COULD NOT INVOKE RIVER GODS TO BECOME LAUREL TREES...

I do not make sound
after Ukrainian artist Sana Shahmuradova Tanska

Female thing

bound

at wrists

by two snakes

or a two-headed snake.

Female thing

kneeling

on the earth

in front of the ghost

of her home.

Female thing

crying

and her tears form

white streams

which is unclean pain,

which is to say that all pain

caused this way is unclean

because it is formed

from violence.

Female thing

is not rigid.

Female thing

defies

corporeal rules.

Woman is

stripped naked

and stretches herself,

wide-eyed,

over her body

to stare at her bindings

python-mouthed

cruel-tongued

My mouth is closed and I do not make a sound. My mouth is closed and I do not make a sound. My mouth is closed and I do not make a sound. I do not make sound. I do not make sound. I do not make sound. I do not make sound. I do not make.

What will you give me for protection?

How long before
the snakes
wrap around
my neck?
How long before
they bite,
before venom
makes me a ghost
and I, invisible, now
can say this is truth
and not a heroic poem,
on a wet afternoon,
in the strength of my bones,
grey agony,
hair loose,
mouth closed?

and I do not make a sound.

I pressed my pencil
to paper
to cry just a pinprick
terror,
a howl
between you and me,
a prayer made of lead
at the same hour,
and said I have come to you,
sorrow,
in this drawing,
in the ruins of my country,
free this line

ACKNOWLEDGEMENTS

Special thanks to Sana Shahmuradova Tanska for sharing her extraordinary artwork and words with me during this time of war and extreme suffering.

Special thanks to Declan Hughes, Sarah Moss, Éireann Lorsung. Jonathan Creasy and Fiona French.

To my classmates and friends at University College Dublin - undying devotion and gratitude!!!

Many thanks to Ciarán O'Rourke for his deep kindness and feedback on the first draft of my collection and the poem "Grief."

To the amazing writers and teachers I have met on social media who have supported my creative practice for years through some very rocky patches.

To Seán Hewitt and the Red Line Festival because winning second place for that poetry competition gave me much needed courage and faith at a very difficult time.

LAY OUT YOUR UNREST

www.ingramcontent.com/pod-product-compliance
Lightning Source LLC
Chambersburg PA
CBHW020217090426
42734CB00008B/1113